Sex and that

'What's happening to me?'
'Am I really normal?'
'Will anyone like me enough to want to go out with me?'
'Mum and Dad don't understand!'
'How far can I go?'

This book answers some of the questions you haven't dared to ask—and some you may not have thought of yet. It explains what is happening as you are growing up. It gives practical help in starting new relationships—and keeping them going. Growing up is about being you. This book helps you to learn to live with your feelings and to discover who you really are.

David Skipp is a practising doctor. Michael Lawson works in pastoral care, and is internationally known as a writer and speaker on counselling issues. Both bring wide experience to this project.

Sex AND that

Taking Charge of Your Life

**Michael Lawson
and
Dr David Skipp**

A LION PAPERBACK
Oxford · Batavia · Sydney

Copyright © 1985 and 1992 Michael Lawson and David Skipp

The authors assert the moral right
to be identified as the authors of this work

Published by
Lion Publishing plc
Sandy Lane West, Oxford, England
ISBN 0 7459 2388 7
Albatross Books Pty Ltd
PO Box 320, Sutherland, NSW 2232, Australia
ISBN 0 7324 0605 6

First edition 1985
Second, revised edition 1992

Picture-strip illustrations by Kim Raymond;
diagrams in chapter 3 by Peter Cornwell

A catalogue record of this book is available
from the British Library

Printed and bound in Great Britain
by Cox & Wyman Ltd, Reading

Contents

This is it (I think)!

Growing up is not just a matter of getting taller! Your body, your mind and your personality are all changing and developing to fit you for the challenge, the joys and responsibilities of adulthood.

Growing up can be exciting. It is also sometimes bewildering—even frightening. It makes you look for answers to important questions which matter to you as a person.

This is the time when boys begin to be attracted to girls, and girls to boys. Relationships really begin to take off. More than ever before, you want to be liked and accepted by others.

You also find yourself suddenly more conscious of your own feelings and needs. You need to find and assert your own identity. You find yourself wanting to question parents and teachers—to ask *why?*—not simply to take their word for things, as you used to.

MOST SATURDAY MORNINGS, JASON PLAYS IN A FIVE-A-SIDE SOCCER TEAM...

NOT AGAIN!

HE HANGS AROUND WITH HIS FRIENDS IN THE AFTERNOON...

AND GOES TO THE YOUTH CLUB IN THE EVENING.

BUT ALL THIS IS ABOUT TO CHANGE...

WHAT'S HER NAME?

OH, THAT'S KAREN

8

KAREN'S TWO CLOSEST FRIENDS ARE RUTH AND ANDI...

MOST SATURDAYS, THEY'RE IN TOWN LOOKING AT CLOTHES, WISHING THEY HAD THE MONEY TO BUY THEM...

SEE YOU OUTSIDE. I'M JUST GETTING A MAGAZINE

HE'S NICE. I WONDER WHO HE IS?

When you first started thinking of members of the opposite sex as being attractive, did you feel:

	No	Yes
Excitement	☐	☐
Heart beating faster	☐	☐
Poor concentration	☐	☐
Blushing	☐	☐
Lack of appetite	☐	☐
Worried about spots	☐	☐
Wanting to please but not knowing how	☐	☐
Concerned about your appearance	☐	☐

If NO: don't worry! You probably will feel some, though not necessarily all, of these at some point.

If YES: don't worry! All these feelings are normal and natural. Adolescence means the transition stage—between being a child and being an adult.

Question point

'Why do I blush?'

Blushing usually occurs when you feel nervous or self-conscious. Feelings like this affect the small blood vessels in the skin, causing them to open up. As they do so, you go red, and maybe feel hot at the same time. But as you relax and become *less* anxious, you gradually stop blushing.

The more you worry about blushing, the worse it gets. The secret is to relax, accept the fact that you *do* blush from time to time—and you'll probably find it isn't as bad as it was. In any case, there is nothing wrong with it. It's absolutely normal.

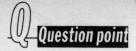

Question point

'What can I do about my spots?'

Spots, acne or zits are very common. This is how they happen. Small glands on the face make an oily substance to keep the skin in good condition. When these glands become blocked, blackheads and boil-like lumps develop. The same condition may also develop on the shoulders and body. Germs sometimes also invade the blocked glands, causing infection and inflammation, and this can lead to scarring of the skin. So what can be done?

SKIN CARE

● Wash regularly with hot water.

● Try not to block up your skin with too much make-up—if you use it.

DIET

Sensible eating will keep you in the best possible health generally. There is no objective evidence that diet helps get rid of acne, but it is a good policy to:

● Eat plenty of fresh vegetables and fruit.

● Avoid fatty foods and cream cakes.

TREATMENT

● An antiseptic or skin cleanser from the chemist will help fight infection.

● If your skin does get infected, you may need antibiotics in tablet or lotion form; these can be prescribed by your doctor.

Question point

'I'm the first boy in my class to be showing signs of growing a beard. Is it really time to start shaving?'

Adolescence is the time when boys begin to grow hair on their faces: left alone, this would develop into a moustache and a beard. However, if boys don't want this to happen, they will need to shave regularly. At the start, shaving once or twice a week may be enough. Later on, they may need to shave every day.

Some men find that an electric razor is easier to use. Others prefer to use an ordinary razor. The choice is yours.

Question point

'Help! I'm a girl, and I'm growing a moustache.'

Not surprisingly, girls don't take kindly to the idea of growing facial hair. However, the changes that take place in the body during adolescence mean that girls may find that they grow extra hair on their faces. If that hair is dark, it may show as a light moustache. There are a variety of creams available from the chemist to deal with it. Some melt the hair away completely. Others bleach it so that it is much less noticeable. These methods need to be used regularly.

The only permanent way to get rid of facial hair is by electrolysis. This needs to be done by a qualified beautician using sterilized equipment. It is very expensive.

Question point

'I hate the shape of my body. No one is ever going to fancy me.'

As your body matures and develops a grown-up shape, you may feel nervous that it does not measure up to some fashion ideal. However, if you take a realistic look around, you'll discover that people come in all shapes and sizes . . . and still go on to be successful and well-liked!

While you're growing up, the most important thing to do is to keep your body healthy. There are several things you can do:

● Eat a balanced diet. Try to include some fresh food every day.

● Exercise. Some activities will get your muscles into good shape, and that will give you a good, athletic figure. Others will increase your stamina: these so-called aerobic activities include jogging, swimming and fast cycling.

● Rest. Try to get enough sleep every night. Eight hours is a good average for many people.

- Take care of yourself. Make sure you keep your hands and skin clean. Remember to clean your teeth, especially before going to bed at night.

These measures won't turn you into a different person; but they'll help you make the best of the person you are.

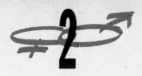

Am I really normal?

We all want to be 'normal'. But you may feel that you are changing so fast and feeling so strange that you wonder if you really are.

The physical changes happening to your body make you want to ask all kinds of questions.

Girls

◆ Why are my periods irregular?

◆ What can be done about period pain?

◆ I'm fat—should I go on a diet?

◆ I sweat a lot—should I use a deodorant?

Boys

◆ Why do I have painful lumps on my chest?

◆ Why do I have pains in my joints?

◆ Why is my voice breaking?

◆ Why am I going hairy?

◆ Why do I sweat so much?

It isn't easy to talk to people about the things that worry you when you are growing up. If you were to pluck up courage, who would you ask, first of all?

Mum or dad ☐ School nurse ☐
Older brother/sister ☐ Doctor ☐

| Friends | ☐ Minister/clergyman | ☐ |
| Teacher | ☐ Youth leader | ☐ |

The important thing is to find someone who will give accurate information, and to have confidence in the person with whom you are talking.

Mum and dad

Some parents are really good at passing on accurate information about physical and sexual matters to their children. Others are not. If you can talk to your parents, they really can help—and they know you better than anyone! Girls usually prefer to talk to mums, and boys to dads, though there is no rule about this.

An open, trusting, caring relationship with your parents is a real 'plus'. It's worth working at, so don't just clam up. They are probably waiting for you to make the first move, or think you know it all already. So try starting the conversation yourself.

Older brother or sister

An older brother or sister who you genuinely trust can be the easiest person to talk to. But, like friends, they aren't experts. They can't be expected to have the right answers to everything.

Friends

A close friend is easy to talk to. But friends don't usually have expert knowledge. And it is all too easy for some perfectly reasonable statement to become totally distorted when it's acquired at third or fourth hand.

Beware of tales that have no basis in fact, such as 'babies are born through their mother's tummy button', or 'masturbation causes blindness'.

The professionals

You may feel you'd sooner die than talk to one of these! But teachers and school nurses, youth leaders, doctors and clergymen are all in different ways expert, trained helpers. They can be very sympathetic and understanding. If you are fortunate enough to know someone in this group whom you regard as a friend, then you are likely to find them very helpful indeed. However, even if you don't know any professionals already, you still have the right to make an appointment to talk to one, just as any grown-up would. It's their job to give you a sympathetic hearing and to provide the information you need. They won't talk behind your back. And they don't shock easily.

When it comes to personal matters, many people feel that they would prefer to talk to someone of the same sex. The professionals will all understand this. If, for example, this means that you would rather speak to a different doctor than your family GP, don't be afraid to ask.

Don't worry about how you begin. It doesn't really matter. You might like to say, 'This is personal,' or 'I feel a bit embarrassed,' to help clue them into the kind of topic you want to raise. Then they'll probably help you come out with the question that's on your mind.

On your own

If you really feel that you have no one you can speak to, don't despair. A reliable, well-written book can also provide much useful information. It may be enough to answer your question. or it may give you the words to help you put together a question you *do* dare to ask.

What a book cannot do is give you the *personal* assurance you need when you are genuinely worried about something.

Here are a couple of questions that embarrass many young people.

'I'm a fourteen year old boy with a problem. Several times I've woken up to find that my pyjama trousers are wet. Am I bed-wetting like a baby, or what?'

For boys, the increasing production of sperm in adolescence can be experienced in what some people call 'wet dreams'. These are perfectly natural. During sleep several things happen to our bodies. For instance, the eyes move rapidly, the muscles may contract and twitch. In boys, the penis may become erect. At this time—and usually connected with the build-up of sexual excitement in a

17

Dr Butler explains what a wet dream is

18

dream—there may be an emission of fluid called semen. At first this is clear but later, when more and more sperm are produced, it becomes thick and white. There is nothing harmful or wrong about wet dreams, and they certainly have nothing to do with bed-wetting. They are the body's natural way of responding to the maturing process which is going on.

Question point

'I'm the only girl in my class who has to wear a bra. People at school tease me that I'll have an enormous bust when I grow up.'

Girls start to develop their female shape at different ages. The fact that your body has started to mature earlier doesn't mean that you'll be abnormally large. Think about some of the women in your family: to some extent you will have inherited a similar body shape.

Whether you think this is good news or bad news, you'll be glad to know that you can learn to make the best of your appearance, so that your kind of figure looks absolutely stunning.

Checkpoint

- When you are worried about something, when you simply want accurate information, or if what you've read isn't adequate, go and talk to someone.

- Choose someone reliable, and in whom you have confidence. Don't bottle up those fears and worries. Chances are, you are quite normal.

What is happening to me?

As you reach adolescence all kinds of changes begin to take place. You begin to look and to feel different. Sometimes it is hard to know what is happening. The changes you can see on the *outside* are all related to changes going on *inside* your body.

If you know all about this already, move on to the next chapter. For those who are still a bit hazy, or who feel there may be gaps, here is a brief summary of what happens, physically, as you grow up.

Body changes: girls

In adolescence the shape of the body changes. A girl's legs become longer, her body lengthens, and she starts to develop the typical female shape. Her waist becomes narrow, her hips are rounded and broader, and the thighs develop pads of fat on the inner and outer sides. These changes occur because of the influence of hormones—chemical messengers—which affect the laying down of fat in the body.

The breasts also develop—an important sign for any girl that she is becoming a woman. Usually, the outer ring of pink skin which surrounds the nipple swells and forms a small mound, and from this, the nipple enlarges. The breasts then increase in size. They contain glands which will produce milk when a woman has a baby. In many cases, one breast is slightly larger than the other. This is perfectly normal: human bodies aren't perfectly symmetrical.

Each month, as the hormones are released into the body, the breasts tend to enlarge slightly. They sometimes become quite painful and feel heavier and the nipple becomes very sensitive.

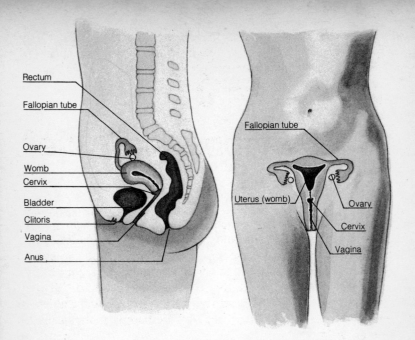

Each time the monthly period (menstruation) occurs (see diagram), the breasts usually lose the tenderness and then the cycle starts again.

A general increase in fat can be very embarrassing, especially when people call it 'puppy fat'. The good news is that the fat is lost after some months, and the body shape alters. So do not despair.

At the time these general changes occur, there is usually a development of hair under the arms and also in the pubic region between the legs, and sometimes girls develop hair on the upper lip. The sweat glands under the arms become more active and secrete more fluid which remains trapped in the hairs, and this gives rise to the characteristic body odour.

Female genital organs

As the hormones start to work on the tissues of the body, fat is laid down over the pubic region. It is here that the pubic hair starts to grow.

Immediately behind and under the pad of fat ('mons pubis') are the 'labia' which is the Latin word for lips. These are two outer lips which are thicker than the two inner lips. Where the labia join at the front, they form a cover or hood and within this lies a small sensitive organ called the 'clitoris'.

The labia surround two openings: one is the outlet from the bladder (where the urine comes from), and behind that is the opening of the vagina. The vagina is a passage about 10 cm long which points upwards and backwards. The opening is protected by a membrane barrier called the 'hymen'. Very often, people will talk about the hymen being torn, or breaking. This sounds very painful but in fact it really means that the membrane stretches. This can occur during exercise, such as cycling or other active sports. It is also stretched during intercourse.

The lining of the vagina is composed of cells which secrete a substance called 'mucus'. This prevents the vagina from becoming dry and also helps stop any infection which may gain access

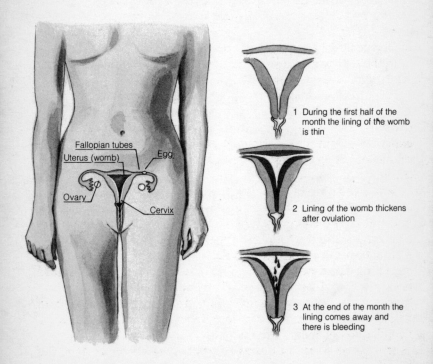

Fallopian tubes
Uterus (womb)
Egg
Ovary
Cervix

1 During the first half of the month the lining of the womb is thin

2 Lining of the womb thickens after ovulation

3 At the end of the month the lining comes away and there is bleeding

to the area. Girls may notice a secretion of mucus, which shows as a creamy-brown stain on their knickers. This is quite normal.

The walls of the vagina are capable of stretching and expanding, and during childbirth the vagina expands in order to allow the baby to be born.

The vagina leads into the womb or 'uterus', and the junction between the uterus and the vagina is called the 'cervix'. The uterus is a muscular organ which develops and thickens during puberty. It is pear-shaped and has at each corner a structure which is called a 'Fallopian tube'. The Fallopian tubes are thin-walled and stretch out towards the ovaries, which are situated on each side of the pelvis.

Ovulation and menstruation

The ovaries contain all the eggs that a girl will shed throughout her fertile life. There are thousands of eggs in each ovary, each no bigger than a pinhead. At puberty, as the ovaries become active, an egg begins to grow and mature and this happens approximately every 28 days. This 28-day cycle is repeated throughout the fertile life of a woman until the late forties or early fifties.

In the first part of this 28-day cycle, the female sex hormone, 'oestrogen', is produced by the ovary.

About the middle of the cycle, the egg is expelled from its ovary—this is called ovulation—and almost immediately it finds its way into one of the Fallopian tubes. Some women experience pain at this time of ovulation. This is due to the release of the egg and some associated bleeding, which irritates the lining of the abdomen.

Small hairs which line the tube waft the egg towards the uterus, and it takes about three days for the egg to travel from one end of the Fallopian tube to the uterus. It is as the egg is travelling along the Fallopian tube that it may be fertilized by a male sperm and a baby conceived.

During the time following the release of the egg, a second hormone called 'progesterone' is made and this stimulates the lining of the uterus, making it thick and safe for an egg to rest in. The glands of the uterus enlarge and there is an increase in blood supplied to the lining of the womb.

If the egg does not become fertilized, at about 25 days the

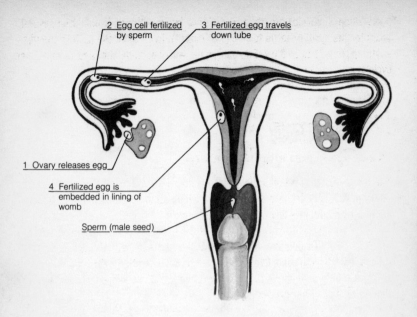

2 Egg cell fertilized by sperm

3 Fertilized egg travels down tube

1 Ovary releases egg

4 Fertilized egg is embedded in lining of womb

Sperm (male seed)

production of hormones by the ovaries is reduced. The lining of the uterus is no longer maintained by the progesterone hormone and it therefore starts to break up and is shed from the uterus along with some blood. This shedding and bleeding is called 'menstruation' and lasts for anything from four to seven days.

It's worth knowing that for the first few cycles, it may be that no egg is released from the ovary. This can make menstruation irregular: it is only as the hormones start to work and the body develops a regular pattern that ovulation occurs every month.

 **Question point**

'What is a period?'

A 'period' is another word for 'menstruation'. Some girls begin their periods as early as ten years old, others as late as fourteen or older. Whenever it happens it is a big moment in a girl's life, as she is beginning to grow into a woman.

Although people talk about 'monthly' periods, because they come roughly every 28 days, periods are often irregular to begin with and it may take several years for the cycle to settle to a regular pattern. Even then, the pattern may be anything from 21 to 35 days. So no girl need worry or think she is abnormal if her cycle varies.

Question point

'How do women cope with the blood loss?'

The blood loss associated with a period is not like a tap turning on—the blood does not rush out. It is a gradual loss, in which quite a small amount of blood—about a teacupful—is lost over four to seven days.

There may be little or no warning of the first period, but this won't cause a problem. The bleeding may be little more than a stain the first time, so there is time to learn how to cope. Even when periods come regularly, for the first hour or so there is only enough blood to slightly stain knickers, so there is still plenty of time to take the right precautions.

Sanitary 'towels' or pads, which are made to absorb blood, are available from all chemists. They have a sticky strip which holds them to knickers so they do not show. These are probably the best choice for a young girl at first, as they are very easy to use. They need to be changed every few hours.

There are also 'tampons' specially designed to be used by younger girls, as well as regular sizes for older women. These are tiny pads which can come with or without a slim cardboard tube. The tube can be slipped into the vagina and then withdrawn, leaving the pad to expand to fill the space. Those tampons without a tube are inserted into the vagina with the fingers. Naturally, tampons stretch the hymen. Tampons have a cord attached, which reaches to the entrance of the vagina, but otherwise there is nothing to show. Girls can even go swimming if they wear a tampon.

Tampons cannot get lost inside, but it is important to change them regularly, every few hours. The tampon is removed by gently pulling on the cord. Girls should make sure they remove the last tampon at the end of their period. Left in for too long, they can cause infections.

A few individuals react very badly to tampons. So-called Toxic Shock Syndrome is a dangerous condition. Any girl who starts feeling unwell when she is wearing a tampon should remove it immediately.

Deodorized towels and 'feminine sprays' give some girls rashes. They are rarely worth the extra expense.

If your first period takes you by surprise, before you have found out all the practicalities, ask Mum or a woman teacher for help. No one will mind, so try not to be embarrassed.

Q Question point

'How do you get rid of a used pad or tampon?'

Tampons *can* be flushed down the toilet. Most pads are called 'flushable', but be warned! Many homes have plumbing which does not take kindly to having pads flushed down the toilet and it may block—so ask first. It is really just as easy to put them in a bin, and if the bin has a plastic liner they can easily be disposed of. In public toilets there is usually an incinerator or special bin for sanitary towels.

Q Question point

'What can be done about painful periods?'

At the time of menstruation, some girls experience pain low down in the stomach because of the cramps caused when the uterus contracts to get rid of the lining. If the pains are severe they may cause sickness or fainting, and they can certainly make you feel very miserable for a few days. Sometimes, just before a period, girls also experience headaches or develop painful breasts. These feelings are caused by the amount of water in the body, which increases at this time.

However, although a period may be a nuisance, it is not an illness. Here are some practical things a girl can do to ease the pain:

● The most important thing is to know what is going on in your body, so that you are not anxious or worried.

● Simple pain-killers will often relieve the pain. But if it is very severe and the cramps make you feel ill and miserable, your doctor will probably be able to give you something stronger to help. There are tablets which can prevent the cramps, rather than just relieving the pain. A warm bath and a hot water bottle can help too.

● Exercise—a good walk or a cycle ride—will often help the pain.

Aside from physical pain, some girls feel rather moody or tense just before their period. They may be snappy for no particular reason or feel very tired. This is known as PMT or pre-menstrual tension. Although many women experience it, it may not occur every month and some women may not have it at all. Every woman learns to cope with periods in her own way.

Body changes: boys

Male hormones ('androgens') are responsible for general changes in a boy's body. He develops (to varying degrees!) the typical male shape of broad shoulders, muscular chest, narrow hips, flat stomach, a small bottom, and well-developed leg, arm and body muscles.

The male hormones are also responsible for the growth of hair on his face, chest, under and on the arms, and also in the pubic region. The reason a boy's voice breaks is that the hormones cause the voice box or 'larynx' to enlarge, and this enlargement causes the vocal cords to lengthen, and so produce a low note. The process of lowering the tone of the voice can take anything from weeks to a few months.

Boys sometimes develop painful lumps under the nipples. This is due to the action of hormones which cause the breast tissue to enlarge. It does not indicate a sex change! It is not unusual and will settle down.

Male sex organs

In boys the testes are organs which produce male hormones and also small cells called 'sperm'. The testes are in a bag of skin called the 'scrotum'. For sperm production to take place, the temperature has to be $1°$ lower than the normal body temperature, which is why the testes are in a pouch outside the body.

The sperm which are made in the testes are minute, tadpole-shaped cells. They have a head and a long tail which lashes furiously and propels the sperm along.

After they have been made in the testes, they travel along a tube until they reach two organs called 'seminal vesicles'. Here they are stored and mixed with a nutritious fluid. They then continue down the tube, which is now surrounded by a gland called the 'prostate gland'. This also manufactures a fluid which provides food for the sperm. The sperm then pass into the penis.

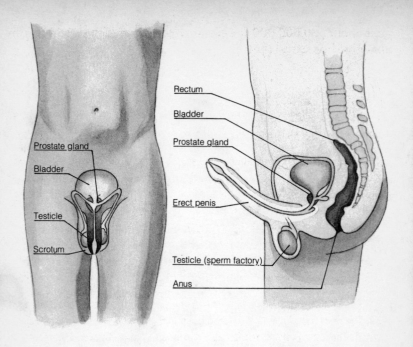

Prostate gland
Bladder
Testicle
Scrotum

Rectum
Bladder
Prostate gland
Erect penis
Testicle (sperm factory)
Anus

The penis is usually limp but is capable of becoming erect. This is because it contains large spaces which are usually empty, but which can rapidly fill with blood and this filling causes the penis to swell and straighten, so becoming erect and hard. During 'ejaculation', the sperm are expelled from the end of the penis.

The end of the penis is called the 'glans'. It is usually covered by a loose fold of skin called the 'foreskin'. This can be removed for various reasons—in an operation called 'circumcision'. Nowadays, the main reason for circumcision is religious—some groups, such as Jews and Muslims, require it to be performed. There are also some medical reasons why circumcision should be performed, but it is becoming a less common operation.

During intercourse, when the erect penis is inserted into the woman's vagina and ejaculation (or release of sperm) occurs, the sperm swim up through the neck of the womb and into the Fallopian tubes. Only one sperm is required to fertilize an egg, but about 300,000,000 sperms are released each time, so you can imagine how small they are!

Question point

'Is masturbation harmful?'

Masturbation is a way of obtaining a pleasurable experience by stimulating the sex organs. In the past, some people said it could cause blindness, others that it could cause insanity. This is simply not true, although there is still quite a lot of misinformation about it.

Boys usually masturbate more than girls and very often the process is accompanied by fantasy concerning girls, or other erotic thoughts.

It is important not to feel guilty or afraid of masturbation and it certainly causes no physical harm. But at the same time we should realize that it is not a fulfilling activity. There are several problems.

Masturbation is habit-forming: this habit can be difficult to break later on in life. The most harmful side of masturbation is the fantasy which so often goes with it. The habit of masturbation also encourages people to live in this fantasy world rather than to find fulfilment through working hard at relationships in the real world.

Some use pornography to stimulate erotic thoughts. Others simply imagine themselves or others in sexual situations. This can lead people to regard others as sex objects, rather than as people in their own right. Our thought life needs to be disciplined, for our own good: we are healthier for cutting out pornography and erotic films.

The Christian view that people were created for the sharing and giving of themselves to another person in a caring, loving relationship makes good sense. It provides a positive reason to reject masturbation as the unsatisfactory activity it is.

4

Swings of mood

The physical changes which are giving a new shape to your body may be difficult to cope with. Even harder, for most people, are the bewildering swings of mood and shifts of feeling they experience.

For girls

You find that you are swept this way and that by strong emotions you haven't felt before. Not so long ago, when you talked about love, it was the way you felt about your parents, or brothers and sisters. Now there are boys—maybe one in particular. You want to please him, to look sophisticated, to look your best.

All of a sudden, looking your best is hard work. You need to take care of a body that is changing from that of a little girl to that of a grown woman. You wonder how much you care about following fashion, and how much you can afford to. You need to take time with yourself, even if it means monopolizing the bathroom.

You are wrapped up in your own activities, often quite unaware and unconcerned about the needs of others around. Some people would say that you are being plain selfish. But in fact you are developing from being just one of the family to being a person who has control over the things that affect you.

For years you have been dependent on parents for everything. Now you have to look after your own hair, buy some of your own clothes—and it's all new to you.

Very often you are moody and unpredictable. One day you feel really happy, laughing and joking. The next you're miserable—unhappy, irritable, rude and unpleasant to your friends. Yet you really can't account for your feelings.

◆ Your body is altering rapidly.

◆ You are becoming more aware of yourself and the effect you have on boys.

◆ You are coming to terms with having periods.

◆ You want to make friends of the opposite sex, but you may be painfully shy and find it hard.

◆ You are developing your own ideas about life—and they may be different from those of your parents and maybe some of your friends.

Sometimes there are so many conflicting emotions that they are overwhelming. You feel you have to shout at someone, or get right away from it all—to go up to your room and play records as loudly as possible!

For boys

You have your problems too. At one time, you would have gone with your friends in a group and you would have had a good time laughing and joking, or playing football. Now there's probably a girlfriend to impress. You want to show her how good you are at sport. You want to dazzle her with your wit!

You feel you've got to wear the right clothes, have the latest haircut.

Underneath, however, you are not quite sure. You don't want to look foolish in front of your friends, and particularly your girlfriend.

The changes in mood and temperament, the ups and downs everyone goes through as part of growing up, are brought on by sudden surges in the hormones being produced by the body. They act on the body to promote physical change and development, but they can also affect your feelings and the way you behave.

Winning through

So how can you cope? How do you handle the swings of mood and emotion? It is very confusing to feel happy one day and miserable the next. It's worrying, in fact. Anxiety then leads to further frustration and outbursts of anger which can sometimes spill over into aggression—towards other people, at home, or at school.

The important thing to realize is that it is not abnormal to have these feelings. They are common to everyone at this particular stage of life.

If you feel anxious or worried that your anger is getting out of hand, *talk* to someone. Try to find out what is causing these

feelings. Many of your friends will be feeling just the same as you.

If at this stage you have a boyfriend or girlfriend, your whole relationship would be less tense, more accepting, if each of you could understand how the other was feeling.

It would also help if you could talk to your parents about how you feel, so that they too could understand what was happening.

Christians believe that, even if you feel you can't talk to anyone else, you *can* talk to God, who made people the way they are and loves them and who promises to help them if they ask him. People who have a relationship with God can tell him how they feel.

Remember to be kind to others, and also to yourself. Not everyone experiences these changes at the same time. Some boys and girls experience the physical change and the changes in attitudes and emotions earlier than others. Again, this is not unusual or abnormal. But it can lead to a lack of understanding of each others' problems, and sometimes boys and girls can be hurt by the comments of their friends.

Some people are more sensitive than others. They can easily be hurt by words that may just seem funny or harmless to you.

In fact we are all sensitive. And because we are sensitive, words can often sting us sharply—even when they aren't true. How do we respond?

When someone says something hurtful, do you:

◆ immediately see red?

◆ lash out in retaliation?

◆ question what has been said?

◆ decide whether it matters?

At this stage in life, feelings go up and down—for some more than others. And it can be uncomfortable. But it is possible to control our reactions. When something is said which hurts you or makes you angry, ask:

◆ Is it true?

◆ Does it matter?

◆ Can I learn something from it?

◆ What am I going to do about it?

If someone says something about the way you look, which you don't like, ask yourself: is what they have said actually true? Does it fit the facts? If it doesn't, don't worry. It was an unpleasant thing to say, but it isn't right. The problem is with the person who said it, not you.

If it is true, and you don't like it, maybe they could have been more sensitive, but perhaps you can learn from it. Is there something you're not prepared to accept about yourself? Is there something you should be doing, that you're neglecting?

So, does it matter? If the comment is wrong, ignore it. If it is right, do something about it.

We all like to get our own back. 'Revenge is sweet . . .' but not really. It only leads to more rows, to deeper hurt. That is the way wars get started.

Jesus, the founder of Christianity, said that it is the peace-makers who are the really happy ones. And refusing to hit back doesn't mean that you are weak and pathetic. It is far harder to be the one who keeps the peace than the one who lashes out.

If we learn to do-as-we-would-be-done-by, we'll find out how to react when other people hurt us—when our moods are up and down, and all over the place . . .

5

Just made for love?

Sex: that all-consuming passion, that all-powerful drive that must be satisfied. If you feel the power of sexual attraction, then you'd do best to give in. The quicker the better, according to popular song.

Is that really the case? It may be true that, if you feel attracted to someone, your feelings make you want to act in a certain way towards them. But there may be some very good reasons why you should put up a bit of a fight, and do what your head tells you is right, because you know that it will be worth it in the end.

You would do as much for a particular hobby. A footballer or a dancer, for example, has to go through some pretty tough training, and they have to get up and work at it even when they feel they'd rather laze around. But because they know what they are aiming for, the hard work is well worth it. And what is more, they know that there is much they can do in practice sessions to influence how they get on in the match, or the dance routine, when it comes to it.

When it comes to sex, it's worth asking the question, what is it all for? Then you can settle in your mind how you're going to handle it, whatever your feelings tell you to do.

Survival

The simple biological answer is that sex provides a mechanism by which we can produce babies and continue the human race. But, although that is true as far as it goes, it is not the *whole* answer by any means. For that we must take some other facts into account.

The way we are made

What we believe about sex will depend very much on our view of life in general.

Are we animals evolving in a world which began by chance? Did all this really happen by accident? Does it carry on through instinct? Should we let this instinct rule our lives?

Or does something inside tell us that we have the ability to choose how we live, and how we use our sexuality? In the relationships of people around us, do we see that some people have made good choices in this respect, and been the winners as a result?

Christians look at the world and see amazing beauty and detail in the natural world, which they believe can only be the work of a Designer, and not the result of chance. They believe that people were made to a pattern laid down by a Creator God. That pattern involves more than physical design. It includes a right way to live.

The Bible's explanation of the creation recorded in the first chapters of Genesis puts it beautifully and simply. God says, 'It is not good for man to be alone.'

We have been designed from the very beginning to be social creatures. 'I will make a companion for man: a helper suited to his needs.' From the very beginning man and woman were made for each other. They are different, but neither is superior. The one is complementary to the other.

This means that we are made both to give and to receive love. Everybody needs to love. Everybody needs to be loved. If we are deprived of love, we feel rejected; we are hurt.

The giving and receiving of love is meant to happen in a wide variety of ways—in families and through friendships, as well as in male–female relationships. Without friendships and love, we experience a deep inner loneliness.

Most of all, we give and receive love in the security and commitment of a permanent relationship—one man, one woman, 'forsaking all other', for life. This is God's pattern for our deepest fulfilment. Built on foundations of self-giving love, trust and mutual respect, marriage can be the source of the richest personal fulfilment humanly available to us.

This is worth savouring. You are growing up in an insecure world. Marriages are not seen as permanent, so homes and families are broken up. People say that sexual relationships outside marriage are OK, that it's all OK as long as you love one another. But they are selling you short!

It doesn't have to be like that. You are being sold short on what love really is, on what it is intended to be.

If you are using sex just to please yourself, you are missing the whole point. If we have been made by God, surely he knows better than anyone else what makes for our fulfilment and happiness? He gave us our capacity for pleasure and enjoyment, so he can't be just a kill-joy!

His recipe—one man, one woman, 'forsaking all other'—is not a sour-faced limitation on our freedom and enjoyment. It could be the best news you have heard yet.

Sex and love

Many people today forget that sex and love are designed to go together. Our big cities are littered with sex shops, selling pornography and showing the kinds of sex films and videos which separate the sexual act from any kind of loving context.

Most of us have strong sexual feelings. Because of that, we need to remind ourselves all the time that sex and love are designed to go together. To concentrate purely on the physical side of sex—to make my own selfish pleasure the goal—makes me less of a person than I am meant to be. It also destroys the beauty and enjoyment of sex as it is really meant to be. It is self-defeating.

What is sexual intercourse?

Intercourse is a climax of actions, from kissing to fondling to physical intimacy. Petting makes you want to go on! This is how it's meant to be—and that's a good reason for not going beyond what you can cope with if you *don't* want to make love.

In the final stages of intercourse the man slips his erect penis into the woman's vagina. After some time, with movement in and out, the man experiences a 'climax', the release of sperm in the fluid called semen. Whether or not the woman experiences a simultaneous climax (orgasm) depends to some extent on the skill and practice of the partners. For both it is a very pleasant release of tension.

Sexual intercourse is basically designed to express intimacy, trust, pleasure, love, between two partners committed to each other in a marriage relationship. It fulfills a partnership at the same time as sealing it. In the rich language of the Bible, two people become 'one flesh'.

Out of this union, this act of love, children are born. Sex is not just to have children. Equally, the possibility of children is not just a risk, something to be guarded against at all costs by means of contraception. Children are meant to be born out of an act of love and union into the security of a permanent relationship.

This union, this sharing in love, has great depths:

◆ **Intimacy** To remove your clothes and explore one another's bodies, apart from being very pleasurable, should be an expression of intimacy—part of the deep sharing of yourself, your life, your hopes, fears and sensitivities with your partner.

◆ **Trust** To trust yourself completely to another person is a tremendous commitment. A warm, caring approach to each other's bodies not only expresses mutual trust—but actually *contributes* to the trust which the one partner has in the other.

◆ **Pleasure** Sexual pleasure is one of the loveliest things humans can enjoy. Intercourse is meant to contribute to the pleasure that each partner has in the other. The Christian view is that sex is a good and beautiful gift from the God who made us, meant to be enjoyed as God intended.

◆ **Love** Beyond everything else, love must be at the centre. Love means tenderness and affection, and a genuine concern and sacrifice for the other's well-being. Sexual intercourse without love—the self-centred 'I want'—is a distortion of how things are meant to be.

The only setting where sexual intercourse and love can develop hand in hand, and where all four of these elements can find a growing expression, is in the one man–one woman relationship, 'forsaking all other', which we call marriage. Wholehearted commitment to one another provides the security and the time which both love and sex need. 'Living together' is marriage without security and often lacks the acceptance and support of family or society.

The changes in you

The changes you have noticed in your body ultimately all help to equip you for adult life—including the possibility of marriage and bringing children into the world. They also help to express your character and personality. You begin to be able to relate to other people in a new way.

This is the point of it all. There *is* a purpose. The belief that we have been designed by God and given a loving framework within which to express our sexuality makes sense. And, if you recognize that purpose, you can contribute to your own future happiness and fulfilment now:

◆ by learning to develop trusting, caring friendships.

◆ by not spoiling things for the future by letting yourself be pressurized into having an experience of sex now, for fear of getting left behind.

Question point

'How do you know if you're in love?'

This question has troubled poets and songwriters, agony aunts and philosophers throughout the ages. In the end, you probably have to decide for yourself. However, there are some things to look for, and to be wary of.

● If your heart beats madly when you think of the person, or you blush and feel giggly when they're around, there's no doubt that they're special to you. But feelings like these are the sign of a 'crush'—infatuation with someone you don't yet know very well. They may not mean that you are really in love.

● If you feel madly, deeply, passionately that you want to have physical contact with someone, to kiss and cuddle, then there's no doubt that you're sexually attracted to them. But, as the chapter explains, sexual attraction is meant to be only a part of love. By itself it's not love.

● If you feel deeply cast down because someone used to take an interest in you but no longer does, you're hurt. It may be that you loved them, but what dominates you is the pain of being rejected.

● If you really care about someone's well-being, and will put yourself out to make sure that their needs are taken care of; and if you are determined to stay loyal to them whatever their mood, then you're on the right track for being in love. It's likely that you'll feel this way about the person you eventually decide to share your life with. You'll probably also feel excited when they're around (at least sometimes) and madly passionate about them (quite often) and cast down if they're unkind to you (but ready to forgive and make up).

Taking charge

Are your sexual feelings strong? Do you sometimes wonder how to cope with them?

Some people have strong sexual feelings. Others don't. There is no need to worry if your feelings aren't strong. We are all different. The way you happen to feel now doesn't mean that you won't eventually develop all *kinds* of relationships.

But what if your sexual feelings are really strong? There is nothing wrong with that: it is what you do about it that matters.

Have you:

◆ wondered how far you can go?

◆ found yourself preoccupied with sexual thoughts?

◆ felt guilty about sex?

◆ been worried or confused about your own sexual feelings?

◆ been concerned about masturbation?

◆ wondered whether petting is OK?

The chances are you answered yes to one or more of these questions! We all *ask* and need *answers* to these important personal issues.

How far can I go?
Put this way, you may be asking two things:

◆ What level of sexual intimacy is right?

◆ Does that exclude sexual intercourse?

Suppose you wanted to buy a birthday present for someone you really love—a member of your family, or a special friend. Would you:

◆ buy the cheapest thing you could find, to save yourself money, time and effort?

◆ buy the nicest thing you could find, which may cost you time, money and effort, but would give most pleasure to the recipient in the end?

If it is for someone special, you will probably want to put thought, effort and some hard cash into finding them a really nice present. The whole idea is to give them pleasure—not to do whatever you find least trouble.

And when it comes to the giving of our bodies, sexually, the same principle applies. When I really love someone I give my body for the benefit and enjoyment of the other person, not for what I can get out of it. At least, that is the way it is *meant* to be. And real happiness and satisfaction comes only when both partners apply this 'giving' principle.

Loving someone means taking on responsibility. We begin to learn to think of their interests and happiness *before* our own. It isn't easy. But it's worth working at. It is when we show someone we really care, that they matter to us, that trust and a deeper friendship begins to develop. Some people never learn this, and their relationships don't get beyond square one—though they may score as far as sexual experience goes. They don't know what they've missed!

So many people get pressurized into sexual activity without being given a chance to consider these other factors. We are giving ourselves that chance now.

There is also a second point to grasp. 'How far I can go?' depends very much on 'how far my relationship has developed'—in terms of friendship, understanding, trust, warmth and love. So, what stage has your relationship reached?

◆ Just met?

- ◆ First date?
- ◆ Going out two weeks?
- ◆ Good friends?
- ◆ Going steady?

We would think it very odd if a married couple expressed their love only by occasionally holding hands. It ought to seem equally odd and inappropriate for a couple who have just met to be climbing into bed together!

It is important to *think first, act second.*

Think about how far your relationship has developed:

- ◆ How deep and genuine is our friendship?
- ◆ How well do we understand each other?
- ◆ How much trust is there between us?
- ◆ Is there tenderness and deep affection in our relationship?

Think about your responsibility to your friend:

- ◆ to contribute positively to his/her well-being;
- ◆ to do nothing which is not in his/her best interest.

There is also a third thing to think of. People have been made in a certain way, whatever they may believe. If they don't live in harmony with the pattern for human life, they will have problems.

Christians put it this way: It was God, our Creator, who gave us our sexuality. He is responsible for the marvellous way our bodies function—male and female. He set us apart from the animals by giving us a means of reproduction which is also the deepest, most pleasurable and exciting expression of love between two people. The physical means of producing offspring is the same, but the level of bonding is different. Sexual intercourse is designed to cement a deep bond: two individuals become one. Once sexual intercourse has taken

JASON AND KAREN HAVE BEEN GOING OUT FOR TWO MONTHS NOW

ONE FRIDAY—

IT'S FOR YOU, JASON. KAREN AGAIN!

JASON, I'VE JUST HEARD THERE'S A DISCO TONIGHT AT THE YOUTH CLUB. ARE YOU GOING TO ASK ME OUT ?!

I'LL PICK YOU UP AT 8 O'CLOCK!

LATER...

COME ON, LET'S GO HOME

AT LAST...

IT LOOKS LIKE MUM AND DAD HAVE GONE TO BED. DO YOU WANT TO COME IN FOR COFFEE?

YES, OKAY

BUT THE COFFEE NEVER GETS MADE

CLICK

SUDDENLY—

GOODNIGHT, JASON—DON'T WORRY, MUM'LL BE ALL RIGHT

I WONDER WHAT WOULD HAVE HAPPENED IF SHE HAD'NT COME IN?

place, we are not the same as we were before—there is a change in the relationship.

That is why God also laid down certain rules—for our good. Sex is meant to be a particularly beautiful and enriching human experience. Like anything special, it is meant to be used in a special way. And if we do not follow the Maker's instructions, we spoil it.

So God gives a great big 'yes' to sex as something good and lovely. He also tells us clearly that sexual intercourse is to be enjoyed exclusively within marriage. That's the whole point of it. It is for two people who are prepared to commit themselves to one another with a promise of faithfulness for as long as they both live. Sex needs to be learned. It may take time—even years—for the girl, especially, fully to enjoy it. This is one reason why the security of long-term partnership is so important.

Sexual intercourse outside this relationship is not only wrong, it is not for our own good. Sleeping with several partners not only cheapens our relationships, but lays us open to serious diseases such as AIDS as well as the risk of pregnancy. In any case, things that are 'instant' are hardly ever the best. God certainly wants the best for us. We can ignore the Maker's instructions but we cannot change the way we have been made.

Three factors to think over:

- the nature of your relationship and what stage it has reached;

- your responsibility to your friend as someone you really care about;

- the Maker's own rules about what is best for us.

When you have thought those over, you are in a position to make some decisions.

Decide now

Brakes on... It is wise to make up your mind beforehand what you are going to do if someone wants you to have sex. You are being strong, not weak if you decide now to say NO. You want to keep that very special giving of yourself for your lifelong partner. Then, when you are faced with a compromising situation, you won't be carried away in the heat of the moment.

When the heat is on

'No' is a very powerful word. Of course there are some people who won't take no for an answer. But if that is the case, do you really want to continue your friendship with them? Are they genuinely taking your feelings and best interests into account, whatever they may say?

You can say: 'When I say "no" it doesn't mean I don't love you, or care for you. It means I have decided to save this special gift for marriage.'

The fact that other people are doing it doesn't make it right. Why should you be forced to be like other people? It is your life. You are responsible for it. And the fact that magazines push it doesn't make it right either. Don't let yourself be pressurized into doing something you don't believe in. A lot of people today are regretting the idea of the 'permissive' society that 'anything goes', or 'it's all right as long as you feel loving and use safety precautions.'

And remember: if anyone ever tries to force you to do more than you want, that person is abusing you. Sadly, there are people—even in positions of responsibility and authority—who do try to use young people for their own sexual pleasure. You are not to blame for what is happening, and you owe it to yourself to take steps to stop it. Tell what is going on to someone you trust and who can help. It may be a doctor, the school nurse, or a teacher or youth leader. This can be the first step to getting the help you deserve to find a way out of a relationship that is hurting you.

Brakes off

Even these days some of us need to be told that we are allowed to kiss and hug! Provided we have a clear decision in our mind about what is right, and how far we will go, we don't need to be afraid of what may happen.

So—how far can you go?

We have said that sexual intercourse is meant for marriage ... but what about 'petting', the whole range of sexual contact from a kiss right up to, but excluding, intercourse?

Between two people who are married it will be the various kinds of sexual contact which may well be completed in intercourse. Outside marriage, it refers to the complete spectrum of sexual contact between two people: kissing, hugging, touching ...

No one can lay down rules. But here are some thoughts:

◆ **Consider your partner** You should never do anything which your partner finds distasteful. You should always be considerate of your partner's feelings. And there should be agreement between you.

◆ **Setting limits** Heavy petting, involving genital contact, is the natural lead-up to intercourse. There is clearly a pressure to go the whole way if heavy petting takes place. Just as it is important to make a decision about intercourse, so it is important to make a decision about heavy petting. Heavy petting is likely to build up pressure and tensions. It may well become a preoccupation which could spoil the relationship at this stage.

Is happiness bed-shaped?

The media, the music business and many others all seem to say that 'happiness is bed-shaped'. This is simply not true. They are selling you short again!

Sex is not the be-all and end-all of life. As part of a good, sharing, warm, trusting marriage relationship, it is a lovely and beautiful thing. But it is not the one path to fulfilment.

Natural curiosity makes us want to find out in practice what it is all about. It is easy to let ourselves be deceived. But the truth is that the quality of our relationship is more important than sexual experience. If we operate that way, our sexual feelings become more manageable, too.

Who is in charge?

If your sexual feelings are strong, how can you stay in control?

Some people so enjoy their sexual thoughts and day-dreams they end up with minds that automatically turn to sexual subjects as soon as they have a moment's rest. They begin by allowing thoughts where they would not allow actions—imagining themselves in a sexual encounter—and they end up wanting to translate those thoughts into actions.

We can't always prevent the thoughts coming. But we are responsible for what we *do* with them. The key to kicking the sexual fantasy habit is deliberately to switch your mind to something else whenever the thoughts come.

Reading pornography, seeing 'video-nasties', hanging out with people whose only topic of conversation is sex, does not satisfy the sexual appetite. It only increases it. So don't just drift. Think about the places you go, the books or magazines you buy, the people you talk with. Keep off drinks that make you lose control of yourself.

It takes strength of character to handle strong feelings. You want to take charge of your feelings, not have your feelings rule you. We are people, not animals! So we have to learn how to say no to ourselves. That way we won't be worried with feelings of guilt. We will be far more healthy, disciplined and integrated people, able to develop good relationships where sex can play an appropriate part, in a relaxed and happy way.

People who are Christians know that the God who made us understands the struggle we have and the pressures we face. They know that if they ask his help, he will give them the strength they need.

'Is sexual intercourse before marriage always wrong?'

When we ask questions about right and wrong, we have first to ask who makes the rules. If, as Christians believe, God makes the rules then, yes, he has made it clear that it *is* wrong. He has made us in a certain way and real happiness for all of us lies in keeping to his rules—with the help he gives.

Sexual intercourse before marriage is also inappropriate. It is meant to cement a relationship—to bind two people together, rather than just being a means of getting pleasure.

But if you have already broken the rule it is not the end of the world. The good news is that God is ready to forgive, and to give a fresh start to anyone who asks him. The hurt can be healed, and new relationships built. The Bible tells us that God's own son, Jesus Christ, died to make that new life possible for every one of us.

'What is oral sex?'

Oral sex doesn't mean talking about it! It is a very intimate form of sexual contact in which one partner uses their mouth and tongue (hence the word 'oral') to stimulate the sexually sensitive areas of the other partner's body, especially the genital regions.

Is it OK, as it doesn't risk pregnancy?

We are talking about an extremely intimate form of contact. In marriage sexual behaviour is as varied in its details as the two personalities involved. Some feel happier with this form of intimacy than others. Oral sex is so deeply personal that it is only suitable for marriage. Like heavy petting, it provides the kind of stimulus which ultimately leads to orgasm. Since orgasm is designed to go with intercourse, oral sex too finds its real place in a committed, loving, caring marriage relationship—where for some it can be a real expression of sensitive care and love. The issue is not the safety factor—whether or not there is a risk of pregnancy—but the intimacy and the level of commitment which should go with it. It is worth knowing, too, that many sexually transmitted diseases can be spread by oral-genital contact.

'Is it important to be a virgin?'

Yes: because it means you are prepared to wait to give yourself to the person who is going to be most special for you—your future husband or wife.

For the girl, there is the added practical factor that premarital intercourse always runs the risk of an unwanted pregnancy—even when contraception is used.

And for the boy it is irresponsible to risk a possible pregnancy and to encourage a girl to give herself physically, when long-term commitment and love are not present.

The fact that AIDS and other sexually transmitted diseases are on the increase among teenagers is a further practical argument against pre-marital intercourse.

To grow up means that you are responsible for your own body. When you were small, your parents did everything for you. Now you are beginning to take charge of your own life—everything from keeping yourself clean and presentable to saying 'no' to things you have decided not to experiment with.

Information point

In some cultural traditions, sex before marriage is considered an important way of checking that a woman is fertile. But what if, having formed the one-flesh relationship, a couple find they cannot bear children? Is it right for the man to throw his partner away? What if it turns out that the man is infertile? The Bible explains that man and woman were both created equal and valuable. A marriage partner is not just a 'thing' to be 'used' to have children. In marriage two persons come together in love and companionship and form a new unit, whether or not there are children.

People need people

So far we have thrown the spotlight on to the sexual side of growing up. But that does not mean that is all there is to it. The physical changes are just a part of the whole process which takes us from being a child to being an adult. Some of the things we have noticed are:

◆ Relationships matter more.

◆ Relationships are growing deeper.

◆ Relationships are developing trust.

We don't want to get so taken up with just one person that we lose out on the whole area of friendships generally. One intense relationship can get in the way of having a lot more fun with others—and it can shut other people out.

So now is the time to develop and benefit from a whole range of relationships. We go through a kind of learning process here, too. We see what happens to others around. We make our own mistakes and learn from them. We gain confidence in ourselves. We learn to give and take.

Sexuality is just part of who we are. It's not just physical. It also affects how we feel, how we think, the sort of people we are.

Each of us is different from everyone else. Our fingerprints are unique. We also have a unique personality. That much is self-evident. Christians believe that people are unique because God has created each one to be a special individual. Why not think some more about that point of view?

It means that you matter. You matter to God because he

AT THE YOUTH CLUB

HEY JASON! I'M TRYING TO ORGANIZE A VOLLEYBALL TEAM FOR SATURDAY. CAN YOU PLAY THEN?

YES, FINE

PAUL BURTON'S ASKED IF HE CAN PLAY TOO. WE'RE ONE SHORT— WHAT DO YOU THINK?

PAUL? DON'T INCLUDE HIM!

WHY NOT?

I CAN'T STAND HIM— NOBODY CAN. HE'S JUST A CREEP!

SO WHAT? I THINK HE'S A GOOD PLAYER—AND IF HE HASN'T GOT ANY FRIENDS LET'S GIVE HIM A CHANCE TO MAKE SOME

SATURDAY. JASON'S TEAM LOST 22-8

ARE YOU CATCHING THE BUS, JASON?

OH, COME ON THEN, PAUL!

created you. And you matter as far as other people are concerned because you have unique qualities. You have a special contribution to make to other people's lives.

◆ Have you ever felt you don't matter?

◆ Have you been worried that you are dull or unattractive?

◆ Have you ever wanted to be like someone else, rather than yourself?

It's a very common feeling if you have. Most of us feel like this now and then. It is particularly common for those in their teens. You might find it surprising but some of the most handsome/attractive/clever/interesting people feel this too!

One very important part of growing up is learning to accept ourselves. We'll certainly want to make the best of ourselves—our abilities, our appearance and so on. But sooner or later we have to come to terms with ourselves, to realize that we cannot be someone else.

The knowledge that God has made each of us a special person in our own right is a real help. We have begun to grow up when we stop bewailing the way we look, or the talents we don't have, and begin to be ourselves. It's not what we can do that counts, but what we are.

We learn to accept ourselves more easily when others accept us, and show their appreciation of us. And other people will show their acceptance of us more easily when we accept them.

Most of us feel insecure at one time or another. We just don't feel confident. We need to be reassured. We need someone to show us some kindness and friendliness. The fact that they accept us helps us gain confidence. Acceptance means:

◆ always looking for people's good points;

◆ being prepared to forgive and forget;

◆ expressing appreciation of others;

◆ offering support and encouragement;

◆ making the other person feel he or she matters.

How could you accept people more—

❖ people at school?

❖ your friends?

❖ members of your family?

 **Checkpoint**

Growing up means that:

● we begin to discover our own identity.

● we learn to be ourselves.

● we become less isolated.

● we enjoy other people's company.

● we begin to learn about the way we relate to others.

● we learn to give as well as take.

● we learn to accept criticism.

8

Them and us

How many times have you had a row about who does what at home?

Sometimes the arguments are serious. Sometimes they blow over very quickly. Small differences of opinion can blow up into major family rows.

As you grow up you begin to exert your own personality and presence more strongly within the family group. You don't want to be told to do something without a good reason. For their part, parents may sometimes become touchy or anxious as they face the changing roles within the family.

Why do parents act the way they do?

Do you reckon your parents are unreasonable, or too strict? Do they think you are selfish, or lazy, or argumentative?

Most parents are very concerned about their children. They feel they have a responsibility to bring them up as best they can. They worry about their children's health and their behaviour. They worry about their chances of doing well at school and what kind of job they will get, if any; or whether they will make it to university or college.

This concern shows itself in various ways. Sometimes parents appear to worry unnecessarily. There is nothing more irritating than having someone constantly saying, 'Make sure you've got your coat done up,' or 'Don't be home late because it's cold.' Is it any of their business to know what's happening at school? Why the homework hasn't been done—hasn't it got to be in by tomorrow?

However, if they don't get a satisfactory answer, they start asking more questions. And often it ends in a row, with everybody angry and frustrated. It is very difficult for parents to find the right balance of concern and understanding without seeming to be always on at you, or just not interested. Instead of criticizing or answering back, try to get at the reason behind their comments and behaviour.

Keep talking!

One of the greatest problems we all have today is lack of communication. It is all too easy to sit down in front of the television and shut out everyone else. Or to go into the bedroom and listen to music with the earphones on, effectively shutting out the rest of the family. Or to spend so many hours playing with the computer that you lose the ability to communicate with other people. If you become annoyed with the computer, you can switch it off. But brothers, sisters and parents are harder to deal with. They cannot be switched off and don't go away.

Getting across

Once people stop talking to each other, their relationships start to break down. If people are not able to talk to each other, or explain the way they feel, they soon find they have stopped talking about anything that matters. They talk only about the trivialities of life.

Without communication, people do not understand what their friends, or brothers and sisters, are thinking, or what their parents feel. Then actions are misinterpreted and there are often arguments. Anger increases.

Communication is one of the most important gifts we have. It is the best way of making friends with your parents, brothers and sisters. So how do we communicate?

We get across to one another in various ways. People explain their feelings and their emotions by talking, or by writing letters. We communicate with each other by our actions. When we are very happy, we smile; we may throw our arms around someone and give them a hug. When we are sad, very often our posture sags and we slump down. We need someone to put an arm around us, so that we can feel their sympathy and affection. When we smile or when we cry, we are communicating our feelings to other people. Every action we make can be interpreted by another member of the family.

Question point

'What is body language?'

You can probably think of some examples of the way that you communicate with other people purely by the use of your body and the way you present yourself.

● Think about the meaning of facial expressions.

- Think of the way you sit or stand when talking with someone, and the way the other person responds. You know what messages are being sent if someone you want to speak to slumps or shuffles or eyes the ceiling. You can begin to work out the kind of messages you are sending. Deep down, you probably already know!

- Think about how much trouble you take with your appearance for different people. It's a compliment if someone has got themselves clean and tidy just for you. It sends a message if someone can't be bothered, or deliberately chooses to shock.

Honestly!

One of the most important factors in communicating or talking to people is honesty. It sounds easy. But it is one of the hardest things of all.

Some people confuse being honest with being rude and forthright and blunt. So, if they don't like someone, they tell them so, to their face. If they disagree with someone else's view, they tell them as strongly as possible.

Other people find it extremely difficult to be honest because it is embarrassing or painful. It is difficult to tell a friend that you are not very happy with something they have said or done. It takes a lot of understanding for one person to be able to tell another that the things they say are offensive, or that their attitudes are wrong.

Both types of people have taken the soft option:

◆ It is easier to be unkind and brutal than it is to be firm and understanding and at the same time honest.

◆ It is easier to smile at someone and hold a pleasant conversation than to say what you know should be said, especially if you allow yourself the luxury of being rude and criticizing behind their back.

We should be careful not to judge others—parents or friends—without looking at our own lives, or our own attitudes. Is there something we need to understand about ourselves? It has been said that you have to understand yourself before you can understand others.

IT'S SATURDAY NIGHT—

I'M OFF NOW, DAD. JASON'S TAKING ME OUT TO THE YOUTH CLUB DISCO

HAVE A GOOD TIME —BUT DON'T BE LATER THAN 10·30

OKAY!

SEX ATTACKER Strikes Again

MEANWHILE...

WE OUGHT TO GO, JASON. IT'S AFTER 10·30!

OKAY, OKAY. WE'LL GO IN A MINUTE

11·20—

However, with this is mind, it is important to learn how to speak honestly and openly, but kindly. It is important that you learn how to listen in the same way. These skills will be of enormous value to you as a grown up, in all your relationships. If you can work on them with members of your own family, you'll be doing everyone a great service.

If your parents take on the hard and responsible job of treating you in the same way, then be glad. Hearing them out is not always easy, but doing so will benefit the whole family.

Checkpoint

● Are there members in your family with whom you have disagreements which need sorting out? Why do you think this is?

● Are there areas in which you could help or change your role within the family? What are they?

● What could you do together as a family to help your communication?

What are friends for?

A ROW WITH MUM...

...THE POURING RAIN...

...AND MISSING THE BUS ISN'T THE BEST WAY TO START THE DAY

HEY, KAREN!

UNTIL YOU MEET YOUR FRIENDS

Everybody needs friends, so they say. It is certainly true that most of us make and develop friendships from the time of our earliest contact with other people. Friendships can go deep. We can also have some real fun together, and be a genuine support when needed. But what are friends *for*?

The answer may seem obvious. Friends are for friendship. Perhaps, though, there is more to it.

Friends do give us support. It is helpful to be listened to when you are angry or anxious. It is also good to have people to do things with. None of us likes to be lonely.

It is not just humans who are social creatures, and like company. There are many animals which seem to go around together in twos or threes or even whole herds! We are like the animals in this respect. But what makes us really different from the animals is our ability to love and be loving. We care in a deep sense about what makes us and our friends tick. We are even able to be unselfish in our behaviour when we want to!

So we are different from the animals in that friendship is one of the qualities which makes human beings genuinely special. The Christian view is that God made us 'in his image', like himself, able to care and share with others. He gave us family, friends and communities. He has done this to help us avoid the painful sense of isolation which loneliness brings to human beings. Friendship is a special gift to us.

Crowd rules OK

It is great to be part of a crowd, so some people think. Others prefer smaller groups of friends. But when it comes to friendship, a crowd can be anything from 2 to 200. Basically you need only one other person around to begin to adopt a *shared* attitude to, say, clothes, music, boy/girlfriends, and so on.

Any group with which we identify, with which we feel at home, whose standards and attitudes we share, is known technically as a 'peer group'.

We all have our peer groups throughout our lives. By and large they are a good thing because they provide us with friendship, support and identity. Sometimes it is just a bunch of friends who hang out together. It may be some special interest group, such as a hockey club. It could be a youth group at church or elsewhere.

Later in life it may be people at work, a group connected with politics or sports, or some other gathering of like-minded people.

However, peer groups can bring their own pressures, by beginning to impose their own standards on everyone around. It's a bit like gang rules. If you don't do what we do, you're out.

Setting standards

So who makes the rules? What do you base your decisions on? Where do our values come from if not from the group?

Ultimately, Christians believe it's God who makes the rules. Not arbitrary rules designed to spoil our fun—more like the 'Maker's Instructions'. Do it this way and everything will work properly. Do it that way, and it will be wrong —it's not the way it has been designed to work.

Telling a lie, for instance, may seem such a small thing. But if we don't know when we are being told the truth, we'll end up not knowing what the truth is at all. Lying is addictive. Once you start it is difficult to stop. God's way, the way society has been designed to work, is by telling the truth.

Trust is a favourite word of the Creator-God. It is needed in all relationships, at home, at school, at work. It is needed in friendships; when you are going out; when you are married. So the sooner we learn trust, by exercising it in our relationships, the better. When the time for marriage comes along, trust and faithfulness are essential. It is that much easier if we have learned to exercise this quality of trust, of commitment, in our other relationships beforehand. So don't be afraid to question other people's standards, especially when they affect your actions.

◆ Do the standards measure up to the 'Maker's Instructions'? The Bible is your source-book for these. Make up your own mind. You are responsible.

◆ Would you want to be treated like that yourself?

Have the courage to say no, if you don't agree. You have everything to gain and nothing to lose.

Try not to worry about what your friends will think if you do take a stand. You may be surprised to find they respect you more. And in any case it is better to live by the truth.

69

Finding friends

Moving back from groups to individual friendships, how do you make friends? Some people say it is all a matter of chemistry. You either click or you don't. There is something in that, but there's more to it.

Even the most outgoing of people often feel shy inside. We feel shy about going up to someone we don't know, or walking into a room full of people, or suggesting to someone that we do something together.

It is a help to realize that everyone is shy to some degree. You won't be the only one whose knees are knocking!

Perhaps you can think of someone who seems to be good at just about everything, with lots of friends, who's very popular.

But do you really have to be good at things to be popular or have friends? Not really: there are two points to bear in mind.

One is about finding aquaintances—the 'sort-of' friends who you like more or less and can usually find something to talk about or do together because you are interested in the same things. To develop a circle of acquaintances, you actually have to identify who you are and what you like! Then as you pursue those interests, aquaintances will come.

The other is about finding friends. Some of these will be people who share at least some of your interests, others may be quite opposite to you. You can offer friendship by making the decision to take an interest in other people, by working at starting conversations, offering practical help, making them feel wanted. Some attempts will feel wasted: people will turn their back through shyness, bad manners, or what could best be described as a mean streak. However, you will receive friendship when some people respond to you.

◆ What kind of person are you? What are your real interests?

◆ What kind of people share these interests? Where can you find them?

◆ What could you do to offer friendship? Can you think of even one thing you would really have the courage to do? Go ahead!

◆ How will you survive if people don't respond? You won't sink through the floor, however much you want to, so there's no harm in thinking of how you will see the situation through to its end.

Question point

'Is there something wrong with me if I don't have a best friend?'

The answer is no. If you do have a best friend, that is fine. It is a real bonus to enjoy a good friendship. If you do have a special friend, don't be exclusive. Be aware of others around you. Make sure you mix: don't isolate yourselves. Otherwise even a good friendship can begin to have negative effects.

It is best all round to have a wide range of friendships. Get to know as many people as possible, though the deepest friendships will be with a smaller circle.

If you find it really hard making friends, even after you've thought about some of the ideas above, do talk to someone. Many people find making friends difficult. There is definitely no shame in that. It is much better to talk about it, than bottle up your worries. Talk to your parents, if you can—or anyone you trust. A good counsellor will be able to help you put together a practical plan for getting to know more people, a plan that takes account of the opportunities (or lack of them) in your area.

And if you still feel left out of the 'inner ring', the group with all the best people in it, don't worry! Be free to be yourself. Try another direction altogether. Who knows, you might be able to start a whole new group of friends of your own.

Question point

'If I am strongly attracted to someone of my own sex, does it mean I am homosexual?'

There is strong attraction between the sexes in adolescence, but there are still good friendships between members of the same sex.

There is often hero worship, too—when a younger boy admires an older one and enjoys being in his company. The older boy may be a good footballer, clever at work, or just particularly nice to the younger one. Very often, the younger boy will want to model himself on the older boy's behaviour. This in itself is not a bad thing—it is a normal phase.

The same thing happens with girls. The younger ones may develop an attachment to an older girl and want to be in her company and do the same sort of things. Again this is normal reaction, and a valuable way of learning, as long as you copy the good points, not the bad!

Both boys and girls go through a period of sexual adjustment during adolescence. Sometimes there may be physical attraction between those of the same sex. This is quite normal. But it is important to avoid physical sexual contact with others of your own sex. This is not how you have been made to behave; it is not God's best for you.

10

Beginning and ending

'How can I get going on my first date?'

'How can I "finish" with someone I don't want to go out with any more?'

'Is anyone really going to like me enough to want to go out with me?'

Sooner or later we all want to know the answers to these questions.

Do you worry about your appearance, or worry what others might think of you? It doesn't really help to say that it doesn't matter *what* other people think (even though it's true!). None of us has perfect looks. And there is a limit to what we can do to get rid of unwanted hair, pimples, spots and the like. In the end it is what you *are* which really counts, not nearly so much how you *look*.

It is true, we all feel self-conscious sometimes— especially when it comes to asking someone out. So how do you get going on that first date?

You have to begin personal contact in some way, and a smile is sometimes the most natural and unthreatening way to go about things. Then a conversation can begin to open up more naturally.

◆ Learn to ask questions.

◆ Learn to listen.

◆ Be interested in the other person. Share something of yourself and what makes you tick.

This is how common ground is established and friendships begin.

Waiting can be frustrating

'The trouble is, Mum, he's been nice to me at school, but I do wish he would ask me out. I bet it's my legs he doesn't like.'

You may be feeling impatient, but what about him? He is talking things over with his friend ...

'She's really nice. But I don't reckon she likes me enough to go out with me. I'll look an awful fool if she says no.'

'You'll never know, if you don't ask ...'

So a week later he finds himself saying, 'Er, some of us want to go and see that new film. Would you like to come?'

'Thanks. I'd like that ...'

Three is not always a crowd

Sometimes it's better to do something with other people around—going as a group to a cinema, roller-skating or swimming. That way you can get to know one another in a more natural, less pressurized way. It also feels safer that way!

Money matters

When the opportunity to go out together does come, it is good sometimes to share expenses. Better still, do things which are either cheap or free. Then there won't be the embarrassment of not being able to do something together because it costs too much.

Try to be open about money. Say at the very beginning if the film will be too expensive for you. Sometimes it is possible to treat one another. These days girls can treat boys, as well as boys girls. But coffee or a coke doesn't cost much, and neither does the local youth club. And a card which you have made yourself may be much nicer than that big plush padded one in a box which costs a fortune! Do you *really* have to impress your friend that much?

Being romantic

What does it actually mean to be romantic? The TV and cinema seem to have got it taped: dinner for two by candlelight—sweet music, and a head waiter who treats the lady like a million dollars. Is it really like that?

Unfortunately there are no rules about being romantic: except perhaps doing whatever your friend enjoys most. And that sometimes does mean giving flowers, or going along with him to the football match. That's much more important than softly-spoken words, or trying to do it like they do on the box. Don't worry about being romantic. Having fun doing things together so you have shared experience is more real. It will also help you to get to know one another.

Be considerate and caring. Be yourself and you'll get it right.

The first kiss?

'I really enjoyed the film. Thanks for inviting me.' She leans over and gives him a peck on the cheek. He summons up courage, and gives her a short, gentle kiss on the lips as they say good-bye.

There are no hard and fast rules about when to kiss—except a genuine respect for one another's wishes and feelings. In some cultures kissing and any sort of physical contact wait for engagement. In others, particularly those conditioned by Western television, the boy in particular is often wanting all he can get first time out!

Taking someone out just as a way of using them is obviously wrong. It's not treating someone as a person at all—just an excuse to satisfy your own animal urges! Don't expect too much too soon. Heavy kissing and petting can become all absorbing. Don't let it spoil the delight of the genuine kiss, the discovery of one another, all the gradual, beautiful stages of growing up. If you try to get all of life's experience into one quick fling, you'll miss the real thing altogether.

Question point

'Does it matter if I don't have a girlfriend or boyfriend?'

No it doesn't. Some people don't have friends like this until much later in life. There's nothing wrong with you if you don't. (See what was said about 'peer group' pressure in chapter 9, for instance.) The important thing for everyone is to try to form good friendships, whether or not they involve boyfriend/girlfriend relationships.

Yes it does. To be fair, if you feel that people in your crowd are all pairing off—all except you, that is—then you're very likely to be bewildered, upset, or even downright angry. You have to hold your nerve, and take care of the friendships that you do have.

Question point

'Is it possible to finish a relationship without everyone getting badly hurt?'

Well it *is* possible. Most boyfriend/girlfriend relationships must come to an end sometime. In general, they are temporary—until of course you find that special person you want to marry.

Some will end by a gradual drifting apart, when both people decide that their friendship is not so special after all.

Others will be ended by one person, leaving the other feeling anything from confused to distraught.

But the *way* to end a relationship needs some thought. If you haven't got too involved physically you can part on good terms, and stay friends. One argument against too much sexual contact is that you can't just undo what the Bible calls becoming 'one flesh' without scars. Fore-warned is fore-armed!

- However difficult the relationship has become, do try to be gentle and respect one another's feelings.

- Don't go in for accusations and recriminations—they achieve nothing.

- Do be sensitive about your timing. It is heartless to call things off just before a major exam or an emotionally important situation.

- Try to remain friends if you can. That way the vacuum created by parting is easier to manage.

- Do talk to friends or family—and to God—about it. Talking helps; and so do the prayers of friends at times like this.

- If you are the one that is left, then you will need the help and support of other friends, and your family, at this time. You may need people to spread the sad news and help bring you back into the social circle again.

SATURDAY MORNING—KAREN TAKES JASON SHOPPING _AGAIN_

KAREN, YOU'RE OBSESSED WITH CLOTHES—THIS IS JUST A WASTE OF A SATURDAY MORNING!

WHAT?

AT LEAST I CARE ABOUT THE WAY I LOOK! I MEAN LOOK AT YOUR SHIRT—DO YOU _SLEEP_ IN IT?

IT DOESN'T MATTER WHAT YOU LOOK LIKE. IT'S WHAT YOU'RE LIKE INSIDE THAT COUNTS

WELL, IF THAT'S TRUE, YOU'RE DEAD SELFISH. ALL YOU WANT TO DO IS PLAY SOCCER AND SEE YOUR *** FRIENDS ALL THE TIME! WHAT ABOUT ME?

79

- Don't blame yourself, and don't start thinking you're a failure just because one person has moved out of your life.

- Don't try to get him or her back. There will be others. Just be patient, someone else will come along.

- Even though you'll feel upset and rejected, many people have been through this and survived. You will too.

Power to love

We need not worry if friendships come and go. After all, being temporary, these relationships give us the chance to get the feel of who we really are. They help us to relate to the opposite sex. Even if you think you have found the person you will eventually marry, enjoy your single years getting to know other people. Give yourself the freedom to put off a final decision until you are older. Even if you don't change your mind, the wider experience of people will enrich your life.

What we need most in all our relationships, whether family, friends or special friendships, is love. Love has many sides to its meaning. But there is no better description of real love than these famous words from the Bible, when the apostle Paul was writing to people he was really concerned about:

'Love is patient and kind; it is not jealous or conceited or proud; love is not ill-mannered or selfish or irritable; love does not keep a record of wrongs; love is not happy with evil, but is happy with the truth. Love never gives up, and its faith, hope, and patience never fail.' (You can look up the whole passage in the Bible—Paul's first letter to the Corinthians, chapter 13, verses 4–7.)

The people to whom Paul wrote had certainly come to know a new power from God which enabled them to put love into action in their relationships. That power came from their personal knowledge of Jesus Christ.

If we look at Jesus' own life, we see someone who really lived out the kind of love Paul describes. He was concerned for everyone with whom he came into contact. He gave himself to others. He was totally unselfish. And today Jesus offers that same power, that same love, to any one of us who genuinely wants to follow him.

This means that it is possible for us to find a new strength from God to help us to live out these same qualities of love in our own relationships. We have only to ask. When we trust our lives to him, Jesus promises us his power to live by—the power to love.

What you've always wanted to ask...

'What is contraception?'

It is the prevention of pregnancy. The aim is for people to be able to plan the size of their families rather than have unwanted children.

'What are the various forms of contraception?'

1. Barriers: these methods include the cap and the sheath.

2. Mechanical methods: for example, a device called a loop or coil inserted into the uterus. These prevent implantation rather than conception.

3. Hormonal methods: the use of hormones to prevent ovulation—the pill.

4. The rhythm method: a way of determining when ovulation has occurred so that intercourse can be avoided at that time of the month.

5. Chemicals: usually used with a barrier method.

Barriers

The cap or diaphragm is a dome-shaped rubber object which is inserted into the vagina and lies over the opening at the neck of the womb. It prevents sperm from gaining entry and fertilizing an egg. The other form of barrier contraceptive, the sheath or condom, is used by the man. It is a tight-fitting rubber sleeve which fits over the penis. Again it aims to prevent sperm, released during intercourse, from getting into the womb and fertilizing an egg. It is the only method that is also effective against AIDS and sexually transmitted diseases, if used properly. It is safe, but not foolproof.

Mechanical methods

The coil is a small piece of plastic, shaped like a 'T', or like a coil spring, which is inserted into the womb. Most have copper added to the plastic. This sets up an irritation in the womb and prevents the implanting of a fertilized egg in the lining. The coil has to be fitted by someone properly qualified in family planning. Normally it is fitted to women who have had children.

Hormonal method

This is usually referred to as 'the pill'. It contains two hormones which act to prevent ovulation (the release of an egg from the ovary).

Before going on the pill, women usually have to attend a clinic for a physical check-up so that someone can explain to them how the pill works. Basically it is a long-term method intended for use within marriage. The pill has to be taken on a regular monthly pattern: it is not designed for casual use!

There is also a 'mini pill', taken every day, which is safer for older women and those who smoke.

There are some women for whom the pill may be medically inappropriate, such as those who suffer from migraine or diabetes or who have a family history of heart disease. The pill can cause side effects and complications: amongst these are venous thrombosis, depression and hypertension. In any event, anyone taking the pill should have regular check-ups with their doctor or family planning clinic, so that any possible problem can be discussed and resolved.

Natural family planning

Many married people who do not want to take the pill or use a mechanical or barrier method use natural family planning. In the past it was thought sufficient to work out at what time of the month the egg was released and to refrain from having intercourse during that period. The technique, however, has been considerably improved; by taking the temperature every day, and by watching for the change in mucus production, a highly accurate prediction of ovulation can be made. It is then possible to determine the days when conception is most likely and least likely. This method has proved reliable when carried out with accuracy and care. Natural family planning is also used when couples are seeking to have a child, and the woman is trying to become pregnant.

What not to believe

It is wise to add that there are several other 'methods' which are either completely unreliable or lacking any basis in fact. Unreliable is the method of the man's withdrawal before ejaculation: this doesn't work because some sperm can be discharged before the climax. Lacking any basis in fact are all kinds of wild stories, such as 'you can't get pregnant the first time,' or 'if you have sex standing up'.

'What about Christians and contraception?'

The only method which has the approval of the Roman Catholic Church is the 'natural' or rhythm method. The Protestant Churches do not have any such ruling.

All Christians agree that having contraceptives available for unmarried people does not change any of the basic arguments for keeping sex for marriage only. These are based on the *purpose* of sex, which is to seal and express the marriage relationship as well as to have children.

'What is abortion?'

Abortion is the ending of a pregnancy. Sometimes a pregnancy ends by itself. This is called a spontaneous abortion, or more commonly a miscarriage. As many as one in five known pregnacies end in this way. The event is deeply upsetting for those couples who were looking forward to having a baby.

In everyday talk, the word abortion more usually refers to ending a pregnancy before twenty-four weeks by medical means. (A full pregnancy lasts thirty-eight weeks.)

'Is it all right to have an abortion?'

This question raises many issues. The actual law on abortion is very important. Although the law in most countries does set out some circumstances in which abortion is *legal*, there are still strict procedures and codes of conduct that must be followed.

But there are moral issues too. Some people regard abortion as an easy solution for a girl who becomes pregnant. There are groups of people who want to see abortion more freely available. They argue that a woman's body is her own property and what she does with it is no one else's business.

This is, of course, a dangerous argument because, however isolated we are, the actions we take always affect someone else. In particular, abortion ends the life of the unborn baby. Also, there are two people involved in starting the pregnancy, and both should be involved in decisions about the future of the pregnancy.

The argument against abortion centres on the fact that abortion involves the taking of a human life. All human life is sacred, including that of the unborn child. Therefore we must question seriously whether we have the right to end life: the life of an unborn infant as much as anyone else. Even though there may be medical reasons why some abortions are needed, this does not make it right to do what vast numbers of people today are doing: using abortion as a form of contraception, and putting an end to a little life for reasons of personal convenience and to evade responsibility.

Also, there are sometimes complications following an abortion. It is thought that approximately 5 per cent of women are unable to conceive again following an abortion. And there are further problems with some women left emotionally or mentally scarred by the experience. It is a mistake to think of abortion as a simple way out. Very few women who have had one would say that they were totally unaffected by the experience.

The only real answer to the problem is not to let it arise.

'What about morning-after methods to stop a pregnancy?'

There are so-called morning-after methods of stopping a pregnancy following unprotected sexual intercourse. They work on the principle that, although fertilization may have taken place, the growing cluster of cells will not yet have had time to implant itself in the lining of the uterus.

The morning-after pill is an extra strong dose of hormones which must be given within a 72-hour period following intercourse to prevent pregnancy. It is only available from a GP or a family planning clinic.

The mechanical devices placed inside the womb work on the principle of preventing implantation anyway. For up to five days following intercourse they can be used as an emergency measure to prevent conception.

Some people argue that these methods are, morally speaking, no more than abortion at a very early stage. Once again, the best solution is not to let an unwanted pregnancy start at all.

'What is porn?'

The dictionary defines pornography as the 'explicit description or exhibition of sexual activity intended to excite or stimulate erotic feelings'—in other words, magazines, books, films or videos specifically designed to excite people sexually and which exploit and dehumanize sex.

There are people who resort to pornographic videos or magazines because they are anxious, or have problems with their own life and they are looking for sexual excitement.

Pornography cheapens attitudes to sexuality and to people. It can put images into our minds which are often difficult to forget. It often increases guilt and anxiety about what is in fact a natural part of life. In the search for ever more excitement, when the ordinary gets boring, pornography has to get more and more lurid, unreal, violent. The human body is a wonderful creation and is to be enjoyed. Pornographic pictures cannot give anyone an understanding of a true loving relationship. Pornography appeals to the physical sense only, as if human beings were no more (perhaps less!) than animals.

'What is homosexuality?'

The term refers to sexual attraction to someone of the same sex, or to a physical relationship between two people of the same sex. When the two people are women, the term 'lesbian' is used to describe their relationship. The word 'gay' is often used to talk about men and women with an openly homosexual life-style.

'Why are some people homosexual?'

No one really knows.

Some people think it is a condition present from birth. Others think that it is maybe the result of an overbearing mother or an absent father. The evidence, however, isn't conclusive.

It is important that anyone who feels that he or she may have homosexual tendencies should be able to talk to someone they trust.

The Bible makes it quite plain that physical homosexual practice is unnatural and wrong. But this is not to condemn people who have a same-sex bias. They should be encouraged to live their lives to the full but, like any other single people, they are required to exercise sexual restraint. Married heterosexuals are also required to exercise restraint by being faithful to one partner. Jesus did not condemn people with problems. Far from it. He offered forgiveness in place of guilt, hope in place of despair, and a place in the new community of the church, where people can accept one another in loving fellowship.

'What is venereal disease?'

Veneral disease, or VD, is now usually referred to as 'sexually transmitted disease'. (AIDS is dealt with in another question.) There are many forms of disease contracted through sexual intercourse. These include gonorrhoea and syphilis. Gonorrhoea is increasing rapidly; syphilis is declining. These diseases can lead to defects in a developing foetus and to infertility.

Gonorrhoea produces a burning pain when urine is passed and there may be a discharge from the penis. Girls often show no symptoms apart from a discharge from the vagina.

Syphilis may give no symptoms at all, or there may be a sore or ulcer in the genital region. If anyone feels at all anxious about any symptoms, he or she should go at once to their own doctor or one of the doctors at a special clinic for a check. These diseases can be treated if they are diagnosed early enough. Obviously, the more people expose themselves to sexual intercourse with different partners, the greater the chance of acquiring these unpleasant diseases.

'What is cancer of the cervix?'

This is disease of the neck of the womb (the cervix). The disease *may* be caused by a virus transmitted during sexual intercourse. There is also some evidence that an early age for first intercourse and the number of sexual partners are factors which may be responsible for disease of the cervix developing later in life.

'What is herpes?'

'Herpes genitalis' is caused by a virus and is passed on by skin contact during intercourse. The virus causes extremely painful small ulcers in the genital region which flare up intermittently. Although the symptoms can be treated, there does not appear, at present, to be any permanent cure for this condition.

'What is AIDS?'

The initials AIDS stand for Acquired Immune Deficiency Syndrome. This extremely serious illness is caused by a virus, called HIV. When a person is 'HIV-positive', the virus attacks the cells in the body which fight disease, leaving a person unprotected against other infections. The sufferer cannot fight off further illness, so death often results, although it may take several years to develop into 'full-blown' AIDS. The AIDS virus is contained in blood, semen and vaginal secretions. In some countries, the disease first became epidemic among practising homosexuals, and drug addicts who injected themselves using needles that had already been used by someone else. However, the virus can be spread in other ways, including heterosexual intercourse with an infected person. In other countries, such as some African countries, the disease has also spread to the wider population. AIDS can put whole families at risk. A pregnant woman, for instance, can pass on HIV to her baby.

Early on, when AIDS was not fully understood, some patients who had blood transfusions caught the virus as a result of receiving contaminated blood. New precautions are now being taken by the medical authorities to prevent this from happening.

The obvious way to minimize the risk of contracting the HIV virus is not to take drugs, 'sleep around' or have casual sex. We do have a choice in some areas.

Nevertheless, the spread of AIDS is making many people worried. Some of the worries are real, many are the result of wrong information. The virus is not spread by contact—for example, by shaking hands or from toilet seats. Nor do you get HIV or AIDS from mouth-to-mouth resuscitation, or the communion cup in church. The biggest worry among teenagers is the possibility of passing the virus on through exchange of saliva in kissing, where one of the partners may be a carrier of HIV, or have AIDS. However, the experts say that this is extremely unlikely. If *you* are worried, on your own account or about someone else, don't be afraid to go directly to your doctor, teacher or some other person qualified to give you accurate information and support.

Governments throughout the world have been issuing warnings about AIDS. Their concern is to limit the spread of a virus which is a major health hazard and for which there is no cure yet in sight. They have concentrated on providing information on 'safe sex'—particularly on urging men to wear a condom during sexual intercourse. This prevents the man's semen from going into the woman's body and also protects him from vaginal fluid.

But AIDS raises bigger questions still. It shows that it is wrong to assume, as very many people have, that we can do what we like in the area of sex and affect no one but ourselves. Many young people are now making 'one sexual partner for life' their choice. Maybe it takes a shock like AIDS to bring us back to this way of thinking. It is not only a 'safe option' but also the best ideal we can choose. It is best for ourselves and best for our children—because this is the way we are designed to live. In the words of one sixteen-year-old boy: 'We're the first generation of people who think that the age of casual sex is dead.'

Sadly, fear of the disease has led some to shun AIDS sufferers. Both those who have AIDS and those who are HIV-positive deserve everyone's sympathy and help, no matter how they may have contracted the virus. We should do all we can to help and support sufferers and their families—whoever they are.

'What are drugs?'

They are substances used in medicines, either alone or mixed with other chemicals. Examples include the following:

◆ Tranquillizers

◆ Barbiturates (sleeping tablets)

◆ Heroin

◆ Cocaine

◆ Cannabis

◆ Alcohol

◆ Nicotine (found in cigarettes)

◆ Solvents (for example, in glue)

'What is drug abuse?'

It is the misuse of drugs, as a short-term way of 'feeling good'. Even a single occasion of drug abuse can do physical or mental damage, and can lead to a quick death—either from the direct effects on the body, or from suicide while the mind is unsettled by the drug.

'Why do people abuse drugs?'

When people feel unhappy, or lonely, or bored, they sometimes take drugs in order to feel happy, or relaxed, or in order to escape from their problems. The effect, however does not last long, and more drugs have to be taken. In this way addiction easily occurs.

'Are drugs really dangerous?'

The simple answer is yes—all drugs are dangerous. Even so-called soft drugs, such as cannabis, can lead to physical damage, and to the need for stronger drugs, such as cocaine and heroin.

Heroin is derived from the poppy plant. It is a highly addictive drug, which is usually taken by injecting into a vein. Taking a drug is called having a 'fix', and several may be taken each day.

Heroin users find that they need more and more of the drug to get the same effect. They also develop a physical craving for it: they are addicted.

Cocaine comes from the coca plant. It is usually sold on the streets as a white powder. It can be injected or inhaled. One form, called crack, is smoked or inhaled as vapour. Cocaine is also a highly addictive drug. Yet although addicts crave their drugs, the substances destroy them.

- **Physical damage.** The drugs affect the users heart, lungs and brain. For example, the heart can beat irregularly, sometimes going so fast that it can no longer cope and stops. Breathing can become difficult and stop.

   The method of injecting carries physical risks. Germs can cause boils or abcesses. Worse, viruses such as HIV may also get into the body, and lead to death.

   People on drugs stop eating. They lose so much weight their body is even more vulnerable, and if they don't have enough drugs they develop stomach cramps, and vomiting.

- **Mental changes.** Heroin and cocaine affect the mind. Users have slow speech and poor concentration. They may get horrible dreams and terrifying hallucinations.

   Addicts also become suspicious, irritable and even violent. They lose control of themselves. These drugs can even cause permanent brain damage.

- **Social changes.** Addicts need money to finance their addiction. Very often they lie and steal to get the money they need.

   Some addicts become aggressive towards family or friends, and then drift into vagrancy and homelessness.

Relatives and friends become bewildered and frightened by the addict's behaviour as their character changes.

The basic message about drugs is this: don't start to take them however harmless they may appear. Always say no.

◆ Physical damage

◆ Mental damage

◆ Social damage

Can you organize some of the bad effects under these headings?

If you know of someone who takes drugs, try to persuade them to talk to a teacher or an adult whom they trust. They will need help.

Are alcohol and cigarettes safe?

People become dependent on alcohol and cigarettes in the same way that they do with heroin or cocaine.

Alcohol is advertised as giving confidence and making people attractive and happy. Certainly, many people enjoy an occasional drink with a meal and suffer no bad effects. However, alcohol makes people drowsy, slow to react and likely to do silly things. Even a small amount of alcohol can affect car drivers, and many people are killed each year because of alcohol-induced accidents.

Never drink alcohol and drive, and never accept a lift from anyone who has been drinking. There is always a safer way home, even if it does seem a bit more of a nuisance at the time.

Cigarettes are also used by people to help them relax. You may hear them say that breathing in the smoke gives a pleasant feeling, but cigarettes are dangerous. The drugs they contain damage the lungs and heart. There is a proven link between cigarette smoking and lung cancer.

These drugs, like the others, are dangerous. They take away the ability to think straight, your self-respect, and they can kill. The best solution is not to start to experiment with them.